I like to look in Miss Wong's Shop.
There are many things to see.

A big drum stands in front of the shop.
I would like to bang on it.
Miss Wong smiles and says that I can.
She lets me use the drum stick.

2

Some things in Miss Wong's shop ring.
Miss Wong lets me ring the bells.
"Ding," go the small bells.
"Dong," go the big bells.

3

4

"You do not ring or bang these," said Miss Wong.
"You hold it like this and strum."
"Twang," go the strings as I strum.

Some things in the shop are long.
"What is this?" I ask Miss Wong.
Miss Wong puffs up her cheeks.
She plays a nice song for me.

5

6 "How do you play this huge thing, Miss Wong?"
"You must be strong to play a tuba," she says.

I like many things in Miss Wong's shop.
But the thing I like best is . . .

8

Miss Wong!